Good Things
You Can Learn

from a Bad Relationship

Ted Meyer

To My Dear Erica,
Love always,
Lydia xoxo

Published by:

SANTA
MONICA
PRESS

Santa Monica Press LLC
P.O. Box 1076
Santa Monica, CA 90406-1076
1-800-784-9553
www.santamonicapress.com
books@santamonicapress.com

Printed in China

Santa Monica Press books are available at special quantity discounts
when purchased in bulk by corporations, organizations, or groups.
Please call our Special Sales department at 1-800-784-9553.

Library of Congress Cataloging-in-Publication Data

Meyer, Ted.
Good things you can learn from a bad relationship / by Ted Meyer.
p. cm.
ISBN 1-891661-45-0
1. Man-woman relationships--Humor.
2. Dating (Social customs)--Humor. I. Title.
HQ801.M545 2004
646.7'7--dc22

2004008646
--

You know who you are.

First impressions
are just that –
first impressions.

Accents only make
someone cute for a
short time.

Never get a tattoo with someone else's name.

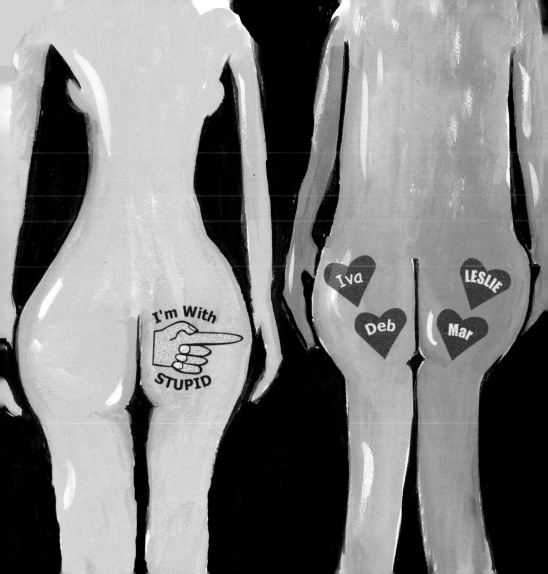

If you make sock logs,
rather than sock balls,
you will not stretch
out your socks.

If you want someone to remember you for the rest of their life, leave them suddenly with no explanation.

Never break up with
someone who has just
completed a course in
assertiveness training.

Opposites attract...

but eventually they wear
each other out.

If someone asks you if their
outfit makes them look fat,
never answer "Yes."

Never date someone
in a band.

When making a peanut butter and jelly sandwich, always spread the peanut butter first, because it is easier to get peanut butter out of the jelly jar than jelly out of the peanut butter jar.

Just because someone
is fun at a party,
doesn't mean they will
be fun at home.

If you date a bartender
you can always find out
what was on <u>Oprah</u>
that afternoon.

A big dog can wreck
a romantic sleep over.

Once someone starts calling the psychic phone lines...

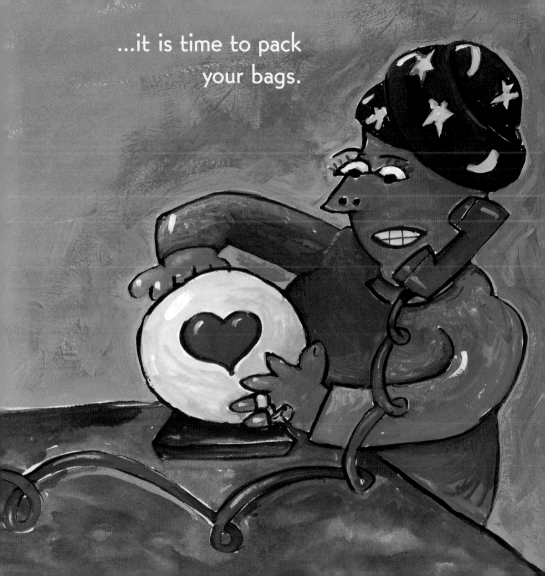

Never date two members
of the same family.

Babies happen.

Love is never so ferocious
as when you believe it
might soon be gone.

Never give anyone
your ATM password.

How Men View Flowers

"What a waste of money."

"They're just gonna die in three days."

"I can't think of a real gift."

"I better get some sex out of this."

How Women View Flowers

"These are so beautiful."

"Isn't he romantic."

"He must have put a lot
of thought into this."

"He is definitely gettin'
some sex out of this."

You won't get your gifts back,
and if you do...change your address.

If you're dating someone who has never used a hammer...it might be time to reconsider.

Never date your neighbor.

Absence makes the heart
grow absent.

When someone says,
"It isn't you, it's me"...it's you.

Once a cheater,
always a cheater.

Sex is not worth the
trouble you have to go
through to get it.

Maybe your ring finger
was the wrong finger
to give someone.

There is always
chemistry on vacation.

Never give anyone your key

unless you are prepared for

unscheduled visits.

If someone tells you they
want you just for sex, chances are
they want you just for sex.

Your true friends will still love you while you are dating a jerk, but you'll probably see much more of them once you are single again.

If someone tells you that you should go to a therapist because you haven't fallen in love with them, you're not going to fall in love with them...so you don't need a therapist.

You should stop and take a moment

to enjoy how good it feels

the first time you use a new toothbrush.

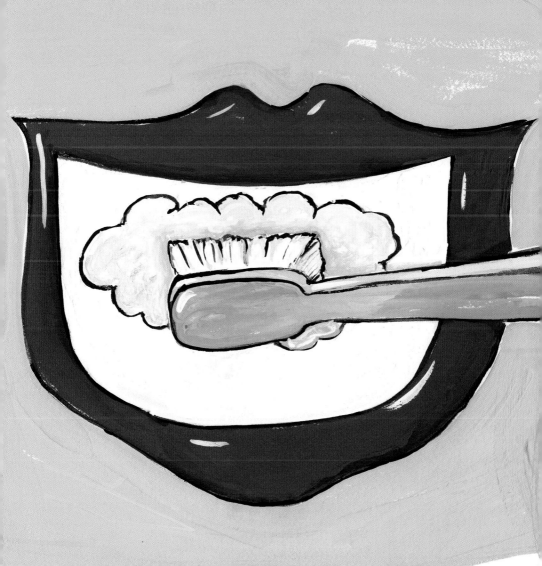

With all the single people available,
there really is no reason to be chasing
someone who is married.

It is all fun and games until

someone forgets to take their meds.

Never date the child

of a lawyer.

They actually make

scissors just for

cutting your toenails.

When someone calls you at 11:00 P.M. to "go out" on a "date," they don't really want to "go out" or "date."

If someone tells you they like
you because you interface well,
they might not be that warm and fuzzy
person you have been looking for.

Some baggage

is okay.

A whole set of

luggage is not.

Too many photos of the

Ex on the fridge

is not a good sign.

Whoever is least into

the relationship

controls the relationship.

You might never learn anything

about your mate,

but you will learn about yourself.

When all is said and done,

you can always write a book.